ADVENTURES
OF
HUGHIE
&
HONEY BEAR

ADVENTURES OF HUGHIE & HONEY BEAR

Boniface Idziak

Illustrated
by
LARRY KULIGOWSKI

BO-GIN ANIMAL NOVELS
Route 1, Box 2
Iron Bridge, Ontario
Canada
P0R 1H0

Copyright © 2009 by Boniface Idziak.

ISBN: Hardcover   978-1-4415-2538-3
       Softcover   978-1-4415-2537-6

All rights reserved. No part of this book may be reproduced or transmitted in any form or by any means, electronic or mechanical, including photocopying, recording, or by any information storage and retrieval system, without permission in writing from the copyright owner.

This is a work of fiction. Names, characters, places and incidents either are the product of the author's imagination or are used fictitiously, and any resemblance to any actual persons, living or dead, events, or locales is entirely coincidental.

First fiction novel of three.

First edition.
This book was printed in the United States of America.

To order additional copies of this book, contact:
Xlibris Corporation
1-888-795-4274
www.Xlibris.com
Orders@Xlibris.com
56881

Table of Contents

Chapter   Page

1   Two Instead Of One 17

2   No Room For Him 19

3   Pancakes And Jam 27

4   I Smell Popcorn 43

5   New Arrivals 57

6   Sheriff Bear Hughie 83

DEDICATION

To my daughter, Madelyn passed away March 3rd, 1995, leaving behind three children, Hugh John, John Paul and lovely daughter Claudia Jean; and her husband John Wables.

Madelyn died of lung cancer and held her pain within. Teaching her children along the path of death that Christ Jesus was taking her away, and soon to a new life.

Madelyn graduated from elementary school in Searchmont, Ontario and spent the remaining part of her life in Grand Rapids, Michigan with her immediate family, Margarite, and her three brothers, Boniface Jr., Stanley Hugh, Patrick Lawrence and her stepsister Jeanne.

Madelyn loved the outdoor life and loved the bears. Madelyn will sadly be missed by all who knew her and especially by her father and stepmother Virginia.

Once she found Christ Jesus, Madelyn went gracefully into his arms, and said goodbye to all her children.

Virginia M. (Rittenhouse) Idziak went into the Lord's Hands August 17, 2003. Virginia was a descendant of Wilhelm Rittenhouse 1644, who was the first Mennonite Bishop in America and built the first paper mill in the American Colonies. The Constitution-Declaration of Independence were written on Rittenhouse paper.

BEAR WARNING!

While "Hughie and Honey Bear" is written for a general audience the young at heart. It is more the less a fictional story since we all know animals do not talk in human language. So this work is from observing animals and actions and reactions over a long period of years.

Bears, as are all wildlife animals in Bo-Gin Animal Novels are not to be treated as one would a tame pet. "All animals that are wildlife are dangerous"—and must not approached to feed or pet! For parents who read to their children this must be firmly emphasized. And teenagers and adults must never, while camping or otherwise, leave food lying around open or leaving garbage out to attract bears, though most times unintentional. For the most part Black Bears have a fear of humans; it is this fear that make a wild animal dangerous, or run or attack! Through his own ability to survive.

In reading Bo-Gin Animal novels I am hoping to touch, perhaps even the most hardened hearts for the sake of preserving animal lives. For animals were put here by GOD for a purpose including to keep nature in balance and it is the job of conservation officers to see animal rights are not abused; as we all should.

* * *

BONIFACE IDZIAK

About the Author;

Born in Grand Rapids, Michigan, author Boniface Idziak became a landed resident of Canada in 1962. He is a self-taught mineralogist and prospector who has dedicated his life to the wilderness and the preservation of nature.

The father of five children (by his first wife, Margarite, now deceased). Mr Idziak is also a proud grandfather of three, and great-grandfather of six. Mr. Idziak currently resides in Iron Bridge, Ontario, Canada with Virginia, his wife of thirty-five years.

This is Boniface Idziak's first published book.

PREFACE

Mr. Boniface Idziak and his wife Virginia became landed immigrants in the year 1961. They were both born in the State of Michigan.

Upon moving to Canada, Boniface took up the profession of an independent prospector in the Searchmont area and they took up residence between Searchmont and Wabos, Ontario. The Idziaks were fortunate enough at the time to purchase a small house from Alex and Dorothy Olar.

Boniface on many occasions has had the opportunity to observe several different types of animals at work and play, while prospecting for minerals in the wilderness country around the area.

Several times in the summer months, they often fed the black bears that came looking for a generous hand out at their residences, with no regrets.

In 1989 while fasting for spiritual help and faith to become a Christian, he received the wisdom to become a poet and author while being in the act of meditation.

Boniface and Virginia both give thanks to the Lord for making it possible to put his ventures and words into story form.

Iron Bridge, Ontario
May 24, 1993

Boniface Idziak

* * *

COMPLEMENTARY

Many thanks to LARRY KULIGOWSKI of Utica, Michigan, U. S. A. for his art illustrations through-out this novel. His time, and his unselfishness is more than appreciated by the author and his wife, Virginia.

My thanks to LAUREL GRAHL of Iron Bridge, Ontario, Canada for typing the camera ready copy for the printing press.

My thanks to my wife, VIRGINIA for her untiring help and encouragement.

* * *

CHAPTER 1

TWO INSTEAD OF ONE

It was early spring and the snow had started to melt on the South side of the mountain range. The droplets started to form small little tiny streams and as the days grew warmer, the streams grew larger and soon the water found its way into the den of mother bear and her cub.

Once the water entered her den, it woke her up with alarm as it penetrated her fur to her skin. She was very surprised to see that as she'd slept throughout the winter months, she'd given birth to a baby male cub, and she adored the little black fuzzy ball of fur as he laid there with his little eyes closed.

Being in the dark after being born he took a good face washing by his mother, which at the present time he didn't care for as her large moist tongue lapped over his tiny face. The only thing he was interested in at the moment was a good meal of milk that his instinct told him was there somewhere, but his mother had moved and it wasn't there where it was supposed to be. After he'd had a good washing, she pawed him over to her breast to get him started on his breakfast, much to his delight.

She herself was very weak and her fat supply all used up from the long winter months. She needed a good meal of green grass or tree buds to clean herself out, but first she had to take care of her new cub before opening the den's entrance so warmth and sunlight could get into the den, the odor was strong, but her joy overcame that. She was as happy as could be, when suddenly she heard a soft whining sound. She pawed around and "Oh My" there was one more little fuzz soft ball of fur, and now she found out she had not just one cub, but two. She now had a sister cub for her little boy cub to grow up with, so she set right to work washing her up too. After doing that she placed her next to her brother with her big paw. Now that the two of them were at their feeding stations, she decided to take a nap.

The entrance was still not open so she had nothing to worry about for the time being, and she fell into a deep sleep after moving up to higher ground in her den. She soon fell into dreamland as she knew that everything was secured and her cubs were being fed. She knew she still had a few more days of slumber yet to conquer before her mate would be looking for her, and since the weather was still cold during the nights there was still time, and then sleep overcame her and conquered her hunger pangs.

These two cubs were her first born, and she never knew of them until she had discovered them upon awakening. With these happy thoughts she now drifted off into dreamland.

* * *

CHAPTER 2

NO ROOM FOR HIM

    The days passed by fast and she now heard someone at her den opening that was still closed, she heard a low growl and then another. She moved as quickly as she could knowing what danger was present, even if it was her own mate coming to awaken her. She moved her two cubs to the back of the den and moved herself to the entrance, and waited for whatever trouble there was going to be, and she was now fully alert.

    As the light broke through the opening of her den, she now saw two black paws tearing away the branches, hay and leaves she had used to close the entrance up before going into hibernation, she was weak but ready for anything to protect her cubs, even against

Her mate the male bear tearing away the branches she placed in front of the den.

her mate. She remembered the time that her mother had to protect her after her father had found out she'd been born, and her mother had turned all her care and affection on her. He'd turned jealous and wanted her out of the way, and would do just about anything to get back his mate, and he had wanted no one to interfere, not even his own cubs.

The minute he broke through the barricade and seen her standing with her paws opened and arms stretched out, he knew something was wrong. All of a sudden the two little cubs began to cry, now he became insanely jealous. He knew before he could have his mate back, he'd have to be rid of the cubs.

"This was not an easy task, it was not like them meeting in the early fall and chumming together," she thought, "This would be a battle he would not forget!" He made a dash to get around her but she then blocked his attempts by stepping in front of him, he quickly jumped to the other side, but with no success.

He then stood up directly in front of her and squared off but she did not want a big battle within the

Mother bear protecting her cubs from her mate who wants to enter the den.

den area and she pounced on him but with little success. Although she was awfully weak, not even her Big Honey Bear was going to harm her darling little cubs.

She knew she had to attack first, and with what little strength she had left she lunged at him with both paws wide open, and boxed his ears and nose quickly. She then got a good hold around his neck area biting with a strong hold and dragged him away from the den, now he knew that she meant business, so he wasn't going to make any more fuss over the cubs, as she boxed his ears and nose once more.

"Enough of this!" he thought, "there are other female bears in the woods that I can chum with," as he ran downward along the cliff side and she let out a couple more loud growls saying, "and don't you come back or else!" As she turned to the den, there were her two little babies looking out, staring, and seeing daylight for the first time. They were rubbing their eyes with their small black paws. Now that she saw them for the first time in the daylight, she knew there was no use in her trying to nap anymore, for they had grown.

Her two baby cubs look out of the entrance of the den at the new world rubbing their eyes.

They were now chubby little cubs who needed more of her milk, but she was almost dry and needed to replenish her supply for them. Slowly she walked over to them and gave them a lick on their ears, then a little cuff to let them know they were not to leave the den while she was gone and after seeing their mother put the run on their father they were going to mind their mother. At least for the time being for they knew nothing of the world outside beyond the den.

They both went inside the den where their mother had left them and cuddled up together for a little snooze, while their mother was out for a dinner of greens and roots, so that they could eat later. Soon she'd have her strength back and be ready to teach her cubs.

* * *

CHAPTER 3

PANCAKES AND JAM

Time was passing fast. She remembered her cubs on first sight were only about six inches in length and now they were over a foot, and weighting about fifteen pounds. She knew they had to have other food besides her breast milk and she decided it was time to ween them, so that they could grow up into bears who were able to take care of themselves.

At the same time another thought occurred to her, "I'd better name them too before taking them away from the den, and if they stray I'll be able to call them back, what shall I name them?" she thought hard. Then it came to her, she remembered an old prospector that use to feed her mother after she'd been born. He'd make the best sourdough pancakes around the Goulais River area, and he was not stingy with maple syrup or his strawberry jam. I use to hear my mother say, "he's the sweetheart of them all!"

I use to hear the mill hands call out to him, "hey Hughie, are you going to town with us for supplies?" And Hughie would holler back, "but let's not buy all that bread as we did before, the bears won't eat it unless you jam it up good." As an afterthought he'd say, "let's get a couple beers this time and a couple for home." They'd smile saying, "okay Hughie, we'll get lots so we don't run out!"

My mother would hear this and say, "we'll have a treat when Hughie gets back, because the next day he'll go prospecting and will likely as not leave a window open, or a door as he's such a trusting person." Then I'd remember when Hughie would drink too many of those brown bottles with the blue labels on them, then he'd get to dancing around and singing as loud as he could sing, the bear went over the mountain to see what he could see. Every bear five miles around could hear him singing, just a laughing and fooling around.

He had a dirt floor in his prospecting cabin and broomed it every day to the solid hard ground. When he went prospecting, we made visits, and drank whatever beer was left around, whether it was spilled on the table or on hard ground in back of the cabin, yes, we felt he was all right with us. He always left for the States before the snow came to stay with his daughter, then ma started looking for a good place to build up a den for her and me for the coming winter.

"Yes, I'll name my cub Hughie, and then I can sing Hughie went over the mountain to see what he could see, that sounds good."

"Now what shall I call my baby girl cub?" she thought. Just then a bee came buzzing around, and thoughts began clicking in her mind. "Sure, why don't I name her Bee?

Oh no! Every time I'd holler Bee, for her then they'd think there were dangers and run further away. I know I'll call her Honey, which sounds sweet. Which reminds me I'll have to sniff out some honey trees so we

Old log cabin by the river, with a window open and a bear looking in. A prospector on the other side of the river panning for gold.

can have a treat. Too much grass is too much gas and besides honey is a healer for what ails you."

"Well look at all the strawberry blooms this year, looks like there will be enough for us too, after all those city folks get done picking and trampling the plants. I wish they were like that old prospector who'd bring his plants all the way from the Sault twenty one miles away, then plant them behind his cabin, at least he never bothered our wild strawberries but left them for us to eat!"

"Well I should get Hughie and Honey down below the cliff and take them down to the creek, and show them how to catch crawfish. This will be a start for them." As they walked down to the creek Hughie wanted to explore on his way down, and his mother had to slap him a couple of times which kept him on track the rest of the day.

Upon arriving at the creek both of them were there. At first looking into the pool of water it so startled them, they jumped backwards, after doing this a few times, they then jumped right in to see just what their mother was chewing on.

The cubs at a pool of water. One looking at herself and the other jumping backwards.

Then they started to feel around the rocks as she was doing, all of a sudden Hughie let out a cry as a crawfish had him by the nose, then it was Honey, she had one on her little paw, shaking it back and forth and the only way to get it off was to bite into it. The taste was strange and not anything like her mother's milk, but the taste told her to dig around for another from around the rocks.

Little Hughie made a pig of himself and he could hardly walk up to higher ground. Once there they cuddled up to their mother's warm fur and had a good sleep under an old birch tree.

The cubs were still sleeping soundly and she could see their paws wiggling as if they were still catching crawfish. Now the next step would be to get a meal of frogs, which was also down the creek and into lower ground, where the marshlands were. She'd do that the next day when they awakened, she herself was having much fun teaching them, as they were in learning. They stayed there all night until dawn, until the morning stillness had been broken with the loudness of the Algoma Central train whistle at the railroad tracks at the Searchmont train station, as the passenger train

One cub with a crawfish pinching its nose and the other cub with a crawfish pinching her paw.

pulled in on its way to a beautiful Agawa Canyon seven hour return excursion trip.

She had no problem waking them, yet they cried as she got up since they weren't entirely weened as yet. She herself was now hungry for a meal of frogs, and she wanted to hurry down to the lowlands before the other bears beat her to it, she'd heard the frogs croaking all night and she knew there would be lots of green leopard frogs there.

That night they stayed near a prospector's house in the valley that made its way to the lowlands, and she'd have Hughie and Honey visit them later in the Fall when the berries were all gone. From the top of the mountain cliff, she could see a lady putting things into a barrel as they had done several times last year, and she'd had a few meals there herself.

As they worked their way down to the swamp, the two little ones of course tried catching grass hoppers, stalling along so she had to cuff them a couple of times until they knew what she wanted for them to do, as they understood this more than her grunts. Once down at the swamp they forgot their hunger and started to play, they were jumping as the frogs were, and were always too late on their jumps to catch the frogs.

This suited mother bear because she was hungry, so she let them go on playing until she'd had her fill of frogs. It didn't take too long and they tired of playing and thought they'd breast feed, but she soon gave them another cuffing, and then showed them how to catch their own dinner, she had enough of the breast feeding the two of them.

Once they'd caught their dinner of frogs, they'd stand on their hind legs and watch the train go by, as people snapped their pictures. Now the Achigan River which flowed along the Algoma Central Railway tracks was not that wide and most times it was low in water, so between rocks in the river bed and low water, it was not too hard to cross over. For a bear it was a good river to catch fish as the water was crystal clear and easy to spot fish on the bottom.

Also on the other side of the tracks was another mountain range just as wide as the one she'd raise the cubs on. Following that range would lead down to old Hughie's log cabin, eight to ten miles away. She knew

Hughie and Honey bear trying to catch frogs. The Frogs seem to be always one jump ahead of them.

Hughie, Honey and Mother Bear waving at the tourist as the train travels to Agawa Canyon.

of several old hollow trees in that range that would be full of wild honey again for the flowers were in bloom, and she could hear and see bees working hard gathering nectar, as they crossed the railroad bed to get to the other range for they'd had their fill of frogs for the day.

Mother bear had her mind on the desert, a good taste of honey would do well if the bees wouldn't get mad about sharing. She wanted to get to an old tree trunk before dark so they could have a good rest and help themselves early in the morning while it was still cool and the bees not too active. As they walked against the breeze, she could smell the aroma of wild sweet honey, what a sweet delicious smell.

She thought to herself, "I guess I'd better not bed us too close to the trunk of the tree, because Hughie and Honey wouldn't get any sleep in the night hours, and they may try and get into the honey, eating a few of the bees along with the honey." She knew this had to be done a certain way and only a mother could teach you, father bears only looks out for themselves and have no time to help their young cubs. She also knew it was

MOTHER BEAR SNIFFING FOR THE AROMA OF WILD HONEY IN THE BREEZE.

a trick to get to the honey without destroying the bees.

They were almost to the honey tree as the smell was getting stronger and stronger, so she decided to stop right there under some fallen pines and rest until morning, then at daybreak they'd get their fill of honey. She almost had the urge to get it then, but Hughie and Honey may get hurt, so she decided to wait until morning. The cubs were restless all night as they smelled something sweet in the air.

As she slept in a dreamy sleep, the trunk of the tree was over flowing with honey and she talked in her sleep saying, "yum yum" and the cubs over hearing this knew that it meant something good was in a store for them! Dawn broke and the bears were on the move to the honey tree.

The trunk was about ten feet in height with a large hole in it and the bees went in and out to deposit their honey, like a person deposits money in a bank. Now the bears were there to make a withdrawal and they never even made a deposit of their own. Hughie and Honey were very excited as the sweetness of the bee's honey grew stronger.

The bees were already up and flying in and around the honey trunk. While the bears had slept a little too long, the mother bear was not going to turn around and leave now as the smell of honey in her nostrils made her more determined than ever, and nothing was going to stop her! As they approached a tree trunk, she poked her paw into the hole and pulled out some honey, a paw full, which she then rubbed into the paws of Hughie and Honey and as they were licking their paws, she grabbed another paw full and stuck it into her mouth, then another and another.

Hughie and Honey enjoyed the sweet sticky stuff, until a group of bees came out in full force, they gathered together for an attack, hitting the bears from all sides. The buzzing sound got louder and louder, and bees were in their ears and eyes and stinging their paws with such force that the cubs were crying for their mother, but she was already on the run.

Once Hughie and Honey got wind of which way she'd went as they also heard her just a grunting as she ran, they followed.

She never remembered there being so many bees there before when she visited this spot with her mother a couple of years before, she got to thinking, "those last two swipes of honey made the bees so angry." Finally she stopped running, and her two little ones caught up to her crying from their bee stings.

They had honey all over their little faces so she licked away the excess honey, then decided to take the cubs down to the river where they could get a drink and cool off in the water. On the way down Hughie and Honey played, licking each other's face.

"That honey sure was good ma!" they hollered out several times.

Hughie asked, "Is that why you call Honey, honey ma?"

Mother replied back, "yes, she is sweet as honey!"

Mother bear helping herself to the honey, for her two cubs.

Hughie then asked another question, "then why didn't you name me frog ma? I like them and like to leap like them!"

"Because I called you Hughie! And soon enough you'll be going over the mountain on your own."

Hughie thought this over a bit, but that didn't seem to mean too much to him. So he dropped any further questioning as he jumped into a pool of river water, splashing away trying to catch a fish for his dinner, but without success.

While in the pool, the sucker fish were on their way up to the spawning headwaters, and their mother showed them how to scoop them up with their paw, and throw them on the bank. After throwing a half dozen fish out of the stream, they went up the bank and had a meal of fresh fish, which were good but now it was nap time for them again.

As the days were passing by Hughie and honey had a lot of memories to dream about, and they both loved it.

* * *

CHAPTER 4

I SMELL POPCORN

It was now nearing late August and the two little cubs had learned a lot from their mother since Spring. Food was starting to get scarce and most of the berries had been picked, although there were a few acorns lying on the ground, so picking wasn't too bad as yet, as there was food in the town dump which other bears and different animals shared.

At times they visited their old den area, and would also watch the lady down below chuck scraps into their garbage barrel, as their den was located just across the road, and about three hundred feet above the level of the house in the side of the cliff.

One evening the prospector's wife decided to make popcorn. The aroma of the large batch drifted out and up with the smell of butter, it smelled so good the three bears couldn't resist the aroma and decided to investigate what she was making.

It wasn't completely dark as yet, but near to it, and so they had their kitchen light on, with the window risen about halfway. As the prospector's wife was popping popcorn, mother bear ambled over to the opened window, and when she put her paw on the screen, it makes a kind of tearing sound although it did not rip the screen. The mother bear made a loud grunting sound as the prospector's wife was pouring the popcorn into a container bowl.

She saw the huge bear staring through the window at her and she let out a loud terrifying scream; popcorn went flying all over her kitchen floor. It scared the mother bear too! All three bears took off on the run, and the kitchen window was slammed shut, as was the kitchen door, which had been open for the evening breeze. The popcorn was cleaned up and put into the

Mother bear investigates the aroma of popcorn coming from the prospector's kitchen.

trash barrel outside, but it had been quite an experience for all involved.

After that first startling experience we bears made many trips to the house for a handout. The humans knew and felt we would not harm them, unless they made an effort to harm us. Even animals know enough not to harm the hand that feeds them. At times the prospector and his wife would come out and feed us, being careful not to get between me and my baby cubs.

We were gone for a while and went to another area where there were a lot of old pine logs and stumps.

There we found plenty of big black ants and sod grubs in the rotten pine wood. This would make us very much fat for winter, and another long hibernation stay in the den.

All cubs usually stay with their mother for two years, or until they are mature enough to care for themselves, as a mother, she didn't mind. Now while they were fatting up on whatever food there was on the dump and flats they had run into a problem. Someone had seen the two cubs and decided to trap them for some zoo. This wasn't easy to do, unless they were very hungry and needed food.

They stayed in the flat lands for a long spell, they had everything they wanted there. There was even a trout stream there, and a backwater from the beaver dams. Even people from the area would drop their garbage in the old gravel pits, if they were on their way fishing or hunting to the back area lakes and streams. Yes, the three bears had a lot of fun in the area while there.

Then one day while up on higher ground on the ridge, they smelled a strange aroma in the air. The mother bear adored the odor, and she headed down the ridge with the two cubs right behind her. They had to cross a beaver pond, then onto the green pasture of the flats. They crossed a small narrow dirt road and she never noticed the fresh tire tracks made by a truck. She was so intent on finding the spoiled meat. She didn't even sniff out the exhaust fumes from the truck.

Little Hughie always lagged behind. He was into everything that he hadn't seen before, so it took longer for him to get anywhere. Honey and her mother always arrived first. As the bears were working their way to the smell of the rotted meat through the trees, mother bear didn't notice that a huge drain tile was among the small spruce trees in time.

When she did spot it, being overly cautious she was not paying any attention to Honey bear. As for Hughie, he lagged far behind as usual. The huge galvanized tile was about five feet in diameter. The one end was two inch wire screens and the entrance had a trap door, which would come tumbling down, should a bear grab the bait.

While she was sniffing the trap out, Honey bear walked right into it, springing the trap door shut! There was not a thing her mother could do, even though she tried rolling it without success, and Honey bear could not get out.

Hughie came running when he heard both of them cry out. Although Hughie had grown there was not much that he'd be able to do. They had done everything they could and soon they would have to give up their efforts in trying to free her. The trap was strongly built, the men experienced and the trap was

Honey bear gets trapped by the conservation officers.

well made. You could break into it, but they soon heard a truck coming and Hughie and mother bear ran for the ridge where it'd be hard to get to, and she knew these two men were not ordinary prospectors looking for rocks, for they had guns tied to their hips which indeed were not prospectors' hammers. Also, they looked to her like dangerous and bad men! For now she felt it was best to stay away, and at least try and save her other cub.

Mother and Hughie watched them from the cliff as they loaded the trap on the back of the truck. Since they hadn't harmed Honey, she thought, "their either taking her to the zoo or another area to mate with another bear to improve the blood line of black bears."

Wherever they were going with Honey bear, both of the cubs cried and cried until the green truck drove away from the area, and were out of sight. Little Hughie hugged his mother very tightly, and now wouldn't leave her side at all. Already he was lonesome for his sister, Honey.

The following day they stayed close to where Honey had been trapped. It was a wretched day as they kept wandering about hoping maybe Honey would escape and come back. But the day came to an end and the sun disappeared in the West.

Hughie huddled up next to his mother that night under a large spruce tree with branches close to the ground.

Throughout the night he could hear his mother whimpering, then he himself cried loudly, so she pulled him close to make him feel safe. He loved the care, but he was still lonesome. The nights were starting to get extra cool, and she and Hughie would have a lot of things to get done before the snow came.

As Hughie laid there, he started to dislike everything about being a bear. He thought, "it won't be the same without Honey around, she was such a loveable sister! I wonder if I'll ever see her again?"

Morning came and the sound of the truck was back, it was coming into the flats where the trap had been set the day before. So both of them ran for the beaver pond, and across the beaver dam running up the ridge to the top, where they could see everything that

Mother bear and cub Hughie on top of cliff looking down at the ministry's pick-up truck and trap.

was taking place below.

They saw the little green truck drive to another spot, which was not too, far from where they'd trapped Honey. The same two men got out of the truck, laughing and talking away.

"We'll get that other little fella before the sun drops in the West," remarked the one.

"Yes, we'll get him all right!"

"Look," responded the other, "his tracks are all over the place!"

They unloaded the trap and baited it with sweet smelling honey, and knew the bears would not turn this meal down. What they didn't know was that the two bears were watching them from up above, only five hundred feet away, and had watched every move that the two men had made since driving to the spot.

As the men were driving away, the one yelled loudly to the other, "we'll come back around the same time, that way we'll likely get the other like we did the female!"

"How wrong they are!" thought Hughie's mother, for she knew she'd now put Hughie first and take her loss, in order to save him. She knew she would have to watch him, as he'd been getting too overly bold a few weeks before they trapped Honey bear.

"The wisest thing to do now," she thought, "is to head for a different mountain range, or take the long way around to the den area." She knew how Hughie loved honey and that he wouldn't be able to resist, for she herself could now smell it and knew in her mind that Hughie didn't have the will power to walk on by the honey in the trap.

She now decided to make the long trip around the mountain range so they could be in the den area, then they could eat at the prospector's place. "His lady was always throwing scraps away! Besides the fishing was good in the Achigan River."

As they left the ridge and flats of hard luck! Hughie was not too anxious to go for he kept on dropping back, and looking toward the area of the trap where the smell of honey was coming from. As he'd get a strong whiff of it in the air he'd cry out and stand on his hind legs.

Hughie's mother had to turn around several times and she would have to cuff him hard enough to make him understand NO! She then kept pushing him in the right direction. Hughie was still growing but in his mind. He was still a baby cub not yet a year old! Mother bear remembered going through the same herself as her childhood came to mind, but she also remembered it in her now mature way, how her mother had given her firm, but loving discipline for her own sake, and she intended to do this with Hughie.

As they slowly wandered over the mountain range, a lot of thoughts entered Hughie's mind. "How come he only saw his dad once at the den? Why were they fighting at the time? Why were humans so mean? Why do they steal our berries, wild plums and wild cherries in the Summer time? Where was my dad when they had taken my sister Honey? Why do humans wear guns? Hey ma, wait a minute I want to know about some things!"

"No! You come right along now, ask me the questions later, we have a ways to go yet, Hughie before we can eat and rest for the night, and we may even move on tonight."

While the way they were going was unfamiliar her instincts told her they were going in the right direction, and that it was safest to travel at night. They stopped and had a dinner of big juicy carpenter ants, which were in an old rotted pine log that had been there for years.

"Ma, how come these ants taste so much like the chocolate candy, we found by the roadside? They sure are good! I wish Honey were here to help me eat some of these ants."

"Well wherever Honey is, we can be sure that she is getting something good to eat," responded mother bear. "Even though we think those two men are cruel, we didn't see or hear them hurt or harm her."

She didn't really know this, but she was saying this because it just might help Hughie through the bad times of the entire ordeal and help him do a little forgetting.

"It's getting close to the time that those bear catchers were likely getting back to the trap area," she thought, "I hope that none of our cousins get trapped."

Her prediction was right. At the scene of the bear napping of Honey, the two men stood over the trap in deep discussion since there was no other bear in the trap, nor were their even tracks around or near the trap.

"I knew we should have used rotten meat in the first place," one was saying.

"No, it's not that," replied the other, "it's getting a little late in the season, and their on the move to get to a winter den."

"We'll just wrap this up for the year, I wouldn't want to be trapped this far back in a heavy snow storm, it's getting dark enough to happen. Look at those snow clouds, heavy and grey, it's a good thing we didn't wait a couple days more, or we'd have had to leave the trap here until Spring."

"You're right," remarked the other, "let's load up and get out of here before it starts to snow."

A thought just came to mind as they were working. Say, do you remember that one old fella? The old bear we could never catch. You don't think these are off springs, do you?

"Oh, I remember all right. We had him cornered once in the old prospector's shack down at the Goulais River. He tore that place up good and when the old prospector came out of the bush, he could hardly stop laughing at us with our torn pants and shirts."

They were both thinking of how the bear had torn up the place, tipping over the stove to get at the stew. It was quite a memory and one said, "No wonder he only has a dirt floor, to keep it from burning down, in all my days I've been after bears, this one really took the cake."

"Whom do you mean, that old prospector Hughie or the old bear?"

The other laughed, they were both hard to handle! As I recall old Hughie passed on, but the old bear, I don't know? Maybe he couldn't do without old Hughie's sour dough pancakes and went above looking for him. At that they both let out a roar of laughter.

It's your fault we never caught him, the other man said. "As far as I'm concerned you never did want to catch the old bear. You'd never set the trap right, not level but on an angle. And not only that he continued, every time the door had sprung shut, he'd already eaten the bait, then there would still be room enough to get his paws under the gate and lift it up."

His partner retorted, "wait a minute, it wasn't my fault it happened that way. Old Hughie, the prospector and he were friends, Hughie always let him out, it's just that we never caught him doing it. And not to change the subject, look at the snow coming down. We had better hurry along."

In the meantime Hughie and his mother were heading faster to get to the den area, for bears dislike the snow especially under their paws. This was the first snow Hughie had ever seen and he was having the time of his life in it. It was something new and kept his mind off his sister Honey.

Upon reaching the den she thought it wouldn't be a bad idea to have another meal before the snow enclosed them entirely for the winter. She had never thought it would come this quickly as it did. So had a couple of humans thought this.

They made their way down the cliff crossing the road into the prospector's yard, heading right for the garbage can which was full, so there was plenty for both of them. Wow! She had never expected such a jack pot for possibly the last meal of the year!

Hughie asked his mother, "did grandpa know the prospector and his lady cook?"

"Yes, all the bears know them, even your dad. That's the talk of the dump these day. We'd better get back to the den Hughie, because we're going to have to pull the door in after us."

"Okay I am, but don't walk so fast, you make me eat a lot more than I could, and I'm over stuffed," said Hughie in trying to put the blame on her for his appetite.

Mother bear and Hughie looking over the 45 gallon drum used as a gragage barrel at the prospector's home below the cliff.

You'd better hurry Hughie, the lady just put the light on, let's just hope they don't come outside. I bet they'll be surprised to find the garbage can empty in the morning until they see our paw tracks.

"I'm on my way ma," replied Hughie.

"Good! Hurry along now, but be careful not to slip on any rocks because they are slippery and wet. We'll be at the den very shortly," she assured him.

A few minutes later they were there, and began raking some sticks and leaves into a pile at the den entrance, which would be pulled in after them to close the den for a cozy winter nap. Their bodies would expel enough heat to keep the den warm no matter how cold it got outside.

While Hughie did try to do his share of the work, he was not a year old yet, so he also played as his mother worked on, he didn't feel any urgency about closing the opening, nor did he feel like he wanted to go into any dreamland. Just before she completed closing the entrance, she heard the sound of a truck motor going by down below the cliff and she recognized that it was the same truck that had taken her baby cub, Honey. She made a growling sound, and closed the entrance up.

While Hughie didn't hear the truck, he did hear his mother's growl. "What are you growling at ma?" he asked.

"It's nothing to be concerned about Hughie, at least not his year any ways," she replied. "Come and lay next to mother, you'll be more comfortable."

As Hughie snuggled up to his mother's warmth, he started to get quite drowsy, and was now ready for his long nap. His mind started to wander through the many events of the summer, of all the fun he'd had, things he'd learned. But somehow all the bad things also came to mind. The men taking his sister. Humans tramping down wild strawberries and blueberry plants. And how good wild plums were and careless humans were to break the small plum trees down. With the thought of how wasteful it was, sleep was taking him into dreamland, as nature was passing into another season for hibernating animals to go, throughout the winter months.

Before dropping off into an almost dead sleep, his last thoughts were to become a bear sheriff and keep wicked and bad people out of the forest of Algoma, which he considered his forest. He would keep all bad things from happening.

The last words heard in the den were, "Good night my dear little cub Hughie," as she tucked him closer to her, "and good night to all the other bears in Algoma!"

*   *   *

CHAPTER 5

NEW ARRIVALS

Spring had arrived and Hughie was awake, but found himself weak and hungry. He was anxious to see his mother wake up and his paw found its way to her shoulder, and he kept on pushing until he heard a grunt from her. He didn't know what kind of grunt it was, peaceful or angry, so just to be on the safe side he laid back down and let out a whimpering kind of sound, a plaintive cry which usually gets mother attention.

Once shaken up, the mother bear sprang to her feet fully alert. She knew Hughie's father would be back this spring to escort her around the forest and other terrain, and her son, Hughie would have to find a life of his own. If his father of course did not show up until fall, then Hughie could roam with her until then.

Hughie had wonderful dreams all winter long, especially about wild honey and all those other edible things a bear would like. He had also dreamed of Honey his sister, and his plan to do something, he would put the run on those two guys.

As he was sitting there in the dark warm den it came to him, his mother had something to tell him, just before falling asleep in the fall she said she'd tell him in the spring. I'd better not ask her now until I get some frogs or honey in me, he thought to himself.

Hughie went to the entrance and started to pull the material away blocking the entrance. His mother watched him at work, for this was the first time he'd ever done this alone. She was weak even though she had not given any birth to cubs, she knew that the speed he was working, he wanted out. "My how he's grown," she thought.

All of a sudden light broke in as the entrance came down, Hughie threw his paws to his eyes, as the sunlight was so bright. The sun was directly in the south, coming right into the den. He slowly opened his eyes. It was so beautiful out!

"Let's go ma!" Hughie was so anxious to find new adventures.

As they worked themselves down the cliff it occurred to her, she had better show Hughie one of the first lessons he must do after waking up. So she looked for a good patch of green grass to clean themselves out, in other words a good spring tonic for whatever ails you, before getting into any rich foods like crawfish or frogs. If he didn't, it could spoil the day for both of us.

"Hughie! Hughie! Wait up for me. I've got something to tell you."

"Hurry mother," Hughie cried out, "I'm hungry."

"Just wait Hughie and follow me, we've got to find some green grass first to heal our stomachs."

"Oh Mother!"

Over here Hughie, here's some tender green to eat and it'll do you good. And when you're out on your own, just remember what I've taught you this year, so listen well to what I'm saying.

"By the way," Hughie remarked, "you said you were going to tell me something this spring, what happened last fall."

"Well at least I see you have a good memory, and when you do pick a mate, you won't forget to come home like your father did," she told him.

"Is that what you were going to tell me?" asked Hughie.

"No! But after we have our fill of grass, I'll tell you."

Hughie never had a first taste of grass before, and once he laid down, he wasn't there too long for he was up and ready to go several times, until he'd finally cleaned himself out good. He really didn't care for this type of meal and thought to himself, "I'd rather have crawfish any day for a meal, if he'd been on his own he wouldn't have eaten it." He remembered the year before, "bears eat honey, it's cows that eat grass so why should he?"

Finally after they'd both settled down, mother said, "remember when we were in the den pulling in the entrance to block the door and you heard me growl, well the reason was I heard that truck going by that those two men had been in, the ones who stole your sister from us. I just had to give them a piece of my mind, son."

"Good!" replied Hughie. "Don't worry ma, I'll look for her, and I'll get even with those two. I'll chase them whenever I see them again."

"You must not bother them son!" she had spoken so abruptly she had his immediate attention. "You'd just get yourself in trouble and remember, the people who carry guns are afraid of us, and you're to stay away from them. The people who don't carry guns aren't afraid of us, and is our friends, they enjoy us. This kind you don't scare or chase, understands?"

"Sort of, ma," answered Hughie in a puzzled way.

Soon they were both snoozing in the warm sun rays shining through a spruce tree, making the bears smell fresh and sweet. Hughie went off into dreamland as he had last fall, but only for a few hours. He dreamed he was standing by the railroad tracks and tourists were tossing square boxes of honey at him and his mother, so that they could take pictures of them. It was such a realistic dream he could even taste the honey squares as he gobbled them down, and woke up choking on a honey square, but it was just a wad of grass he hadn't chewed up enough.

His mother heard him choking and remarked, "the next time you eat grass, you'll chew it well, like a cow does."

"Do I look like a black cow?" Hughie remarked.

"No, we have paws and cows have hoofs, and besides we don't have any horns on our head. If we did, they'd say, there goes another one of those bearhorns."

Jokingly Hughie responded, "and they don't say there's one of those cowhorns eating grass either."

"Oh forget it, Hughie." She replied, "it makes no difference, but a little fresh grass is good for you, you'll see tomorrow, you'll want more of it."

"Oh sure!" Though Hughie, as he had to get up and go again.

She'd shown him a good tonic which he wasn't in love with right now, but as he grew older he'd need it, and found his very own good grass patches she knew. She thought they were in a good place both to rest and clean their system out before getting into a crawfish dinner. As for frogs it was too early in the season.

"I know what we can do ma, can we go to the train tracks to see those people on the train?"

"I'm sorry Hughie, but it's too early in the season yet."

A disappointed Hughie shrugged his shoulders, "I might as well go back to sleep, there's nothing to do!" So he did sleep for a bit longer, and the cramps in his tummy disappeared. When he awoke, he was ready to go fishing down to the Perry Creek.

He awoke his mother and they were off to the Perry Creek to try their luck. One thing about bears they need no net or fishing pole nor bait as their paw is like a built in tackle box with everything there, they need. On the way they met other bears who had the same idea, and some already had gotten their fill as one could see by the spawn on their fur and face.

Hughie thought he'd spotted his sister down by the brook, but he was wrong for he went over to her to have a closer look but no, it wasn't his sister. She made a deep growling sound at him, telling him, "wander off and mind your own business," and as he walked away he looked back, she had stopped eating and of course was watching him. He decided not to bother her again until he himself had caught some fish and had eaten them.

He went back to where his mother was in the creek bed and of course she'd seen Hughie talking to her, and getting the run put on him.

"Mother, that's not Honey bear, she growled at me hard. I don't think she wants to be friends with me either!"

"Well Hughie, her hunger comes first, and later this spring you'll meet her again, just have patience and you'll see."

The fishing was excellent and they stayed there until they'd gotten their fill. Night came and they retired to the den.

Most of the spring they hung around the den area and they had plenty to eat, every now and again they'd drop in on the prospector and his wife. They seemed to have lots to throw away or else they took it upon themselves to feed the bears in the area.

The prospector's wife got to know and love the bears, while we'd be in the yard she'd throw bread or whatever leftovers she had left out to us, but she was careful, whenever a mother bear had a cub or two with her. She knew she had to be careful because it wasn't always the same bear family who came to visit for a quick meal. Her husband without realizing would sometimes step out into the yard and accidentally find himself between us; we smelled no danger from him. The view of their yard was a beautiful sight to see from the cliff we were on and we could see the deposits of food being made in the outside garbage container. It was like having your own bank and restaurant all in one.

The days were going fast and Hughie was growing into a very handsome male bear with his thick black coat of fur. She was very proud of him. She knew he'd soon get into trouble if he didn't find a mate soon to travel with him, for he could be a pushy kid bear when he wanted to be, and this wasn't good when it came to being in bear hunting country.

The Achigan River seemed to be his favorite spot where the tourist train travelled next to it. The Algoma Central passenger trains when pulling out of Searchmont wouldn't be travelling fast, and as Hughie knew from the year before, tourists would want pictures of them as they travelled by, then they'd toss candy and half-eaten fruit out to them and both enjoyed them.

Even the Algoma Central Railway cars and engines had the black bear emblems painted on them. When Hughie first seen this, he thought it was a bear riding the rails.

He'd say, "hey ma! Here comes that bear train

A TRAIN GOES BY WITH A BEAR EMBLEM PAINTED ON EACH BOX CAR.

again with all those bears on it and those nice people with good things to toss out at us again."

There wouldn't be days go by that he didn't mention the train or look toward the railway tracks.

Now Hughie had a dream that people were throwing boxes of honey at him when he performed tricks, and when he awoke this gave him something to think about. Maybe he would try learning a few good tricks, which he did. The first few times he did get a little more candy then the other, but word got about that he was a big show off! Then too, his mother worried that he would get worms from having such a sweet tooth.

She also thought he'd get to be too well known acting up as he did, and the two trappers would hear about him and try somehow to get their culvert trap down to the Achigan River, though she knew it would be a difficult thing to do unless they travelled the rail tracks.

She also knew they'd need permission from Algoma Central Railroad Officials, "which she didn't think would happen." So he might just be safe, but only doing his tricks there, not in places accessible to vehicles. He seemed to be getting his fill of the sweets and candy, forgetting the honey trunk on Goulais River.

One morning he had a surprise! There was a girl bear his age at the crossing on the Achigan River, yes it was the same girl bear he'd met pike fishing on the Perry Creek where the mouth of the creek empties into the Goulais River just above Searchmont.

Hughie was speechless for a few minutes. There she stood on the side of the river. Where tourist tossed their treats to the bears.

Soon the train would be pulling out of Searchmont and he found himself on the opposite side of the Achigan River, however they'd be watching her instead of him, and throwing all their treats on her side, "unless I can get their attention!" he thought, "by doing extra special tricks."

Hughie had to do some fast thinking and his mother was not going to help him this time. Knowing that he was old enough to be on his own, she found her chance to leave him, she had taught him everything she knew, so he could survive.

And now there was a girl bear his age, and mother bear had also taken off on her own, running into the swamp, well hid by the cattails. Hughie turned his head to where she had been but she was not there. He let out a few cries thinking to search for her, but as he turned around he slipped on the rocks that he was standing on, and fell into the water.

The girl bear standing on the other side thought he wanted to play, so she jumped right in after him. Hughie was trying to climb up the bank to find his mother, and she kept pulling him back into the pool. At that moment the train was moving by and the delighted tourist, thinking they were playing, threw all kinds of goodies from the platforms of the passengers' cars.

Seeing this, they both got out of the pool and ran to the tracks together. This would be the start of a whole new life for both of them.

Hughie found he didn't mind sharing at all. He had even forgotten his mother had left him, a day which

Hughie and his future mate (Bow) looking at each other in amaze while Hughie's mother gets a chance to leave him.

he'd previously dreaded to face. Now it wasn't so bad after all. He found a large pine tree and sat down for a rest, but soon fell into a restful sleep. The day was more than enough for him. He had never expected a full day of events to occur that he would experience.

It was the girl bear who decided to be Hughie's mate and she found a soft spot next to him to lie down. When he awoke, he was surprised to see her there, but at the same time was happy not to be alone. When she awoke, she nudged Hughie and licked him on the arm and this made him happy, so he licked her ear as well, the two of them were meant for each other which they both now realized.

Hughie began to size her up and he liked what he saw, it was like two teenagers meeting for the first time at a school picnic or dance. Hughie had proven himself a good dancer just by the response of the tourists, who'd thrown fruit and candy to him and his mother.

Hughie asked her, "do you want to go hunting berries with me?" but he felt so shy and self conscious.

But she liked that idea by answering, "the blossoms are not yet out, so strawberries won't be ripe for a while yet."

Hughie knew he'd made his first blunder. Of course he knew berries weren't mature yet, but he was excited and not thinking at the time. His heart was still pounding from the ear licking she'd given him, his mother used to wash his ears for him but nothing like that.

He smiled when he looked at her, and she smiled back and it seemed they'd accepted each other and would now explore the area together. Hughie didn't want to go to the area his mother was at, she might just change her mind and want him to come back. After meeting his love he didn't want to give her up now for any reason.

Hughie now asked her what her name was and she said it was "Rainbow."

"Why did they name you Rainbow?" he asked her.

She shyly answered, "because when I was born the skies were all different colors."

"Why were you born under open sky?" he questioned.

She let out a little giggle, "how would I know, I couldn't see anything when I was born, I was only six inches long!" Then in earnest she replied, "I only know what I was told."

"Can I call you Bow, short for Rainbow?" he asked her.

"Sure Hughie, that's cute! It's odd my mother never thought of it, but yes, I like it!"

"What shall we do today?" Bow asked Hughie.

"Let's go and find some honey trees of our own," he said. "Those hills look good to me, and there not too, far from the railroad tracks Bow. I know there's lots of clover and wild flowers growing on the side of the track bedding so there is got to be lots of bees there somewhere in a dead tree."

"How will we find the honey tree?"

Hughie told her, "we'll just follow the bees when they go to bank their honey, simple, eh?"

"Sounds good to me," she replied, "we'll see what a good honey hunter you are."

Okay, let's spring to it! Showing more enthusiasm than he felt, just as if he knew what he was doing. Before he had always relied on his mother when it came to finding best spots.

Of course Bow knew the area better, since she had been also raised in this area, but she decided she wouldn't interfere for now and would let him show her what he knew. Even though it was the female who was the provider in the family.

They slowly ambled along the railroad bed, catching butterflies and nipping at a few plants they knew to be tasty. They were just enjoying themselves and their new friendship.

Hughie wanted to please Bow very much, but wasn't paying attention what he was doing. He heard a swarm of bees in flight, but did not see them as he ran toward the buzzing he'd heard, in doing so he ran smack into a hornet's nest built close to the ground. He reared up on his back legs, giving out a loud crying sound as he headed for the Achigan River.

He ran right on past Bow jumping into the water to hide away from the hornets. "At least Hughie knew enough to do that," she thought, and she couldn't help but laugh out loud. It was a funny sight. The hornets didn't bother her, but were just after Hughie.

Hughie cried out, "what are you laughing about Bow, it's not funny to get stung by hornets."

"How well I know," replied Bow, "I walked into the same situation myself a few days ago." Then they both started laughing. Bow then jumped into the water and tossed a fish upon the bank, she then climbed out and ate the fish. Hughie got himself out of the water, and was looking for the fish Bow caught, but she had already eaten it. He turned his head to look at her but there was no eye contact for she was already walking up the gravel road.

Hughie runs into a hornet's nest while looking for wild honey trees.

"She has a lot of nerve to eat the whole fish, and if she wanted the entire fish, why didn't she throw me out one," he thought and felt kind of peeved. Just then she turned around and hollered to him, "hurry Hughie, we want to get there before it's too late, if we want to find a lot of honey."

Boy, she sure is a know it all, he thought, "but I might as well go along with her on this one, and find out how much, if I can, she really does know. She acts a lot like a mother who knew everything there was to know in the bear digest! I must have had a smart father to teach her all the things she taught me."

"Now this girl Bow wants to show me where the honey trees are, what a laugh. I'll find one before she does, she doesn't know it yet but I can smell honey a long way off, if the wind is blowing right."

Just then Bow yelled back, "I hear the hornets coming," as Hughie started to run toward her.

"I don't see or hear any hornets!" he asked questionably.

"I was only fooling," she said, "to make you hurry along if you don't mind!" she continued. "Hughie, look up there, sees that tree covered with honey bees? Well if we wait until morning the bees will be gathering more honey and we can help ourselves to all the honey we want. Only a few guards will sting us, and it will be worth it!"

"That's okay with me Bow, whatever you say," he responded.

By the way Bow, I'm hungry and can't wait until morning, so I'm going down to the river to catch a fish for me to eat now. If you recall, you never shared to one you caught on the river bank. It was such a big one I didn't think you could eat the whole fish.

"Well I did, and I thought to be the man bear that you are, I just thought you were capable of catching your own!"

Hughie didn't know if she was praising him or berating him, however this ended that conversation.

They found a good place to rest for the night after Hughie had caught his meal of fish. He still felt kind of put out because Bow hadn't shared with him like his sister use to do. Morning came and the bright sun rays were shining down upon them with a lot of warmth, and Hughie felt a little better inside.

After waking up and getting the sleep out of their eyes he heard a loud buzzing sound. It was a swarm of honey bees flying over head on their way to collect more honey. Hughie was delighted, jumping up and down, ready to attack the honey tree. Bow joined in making a happy little dance with him, everything was as Bow had predicted.

It didn't take long. Hughie was up in the tree helping himself to the honey. As he stuck his paw into the hole grabbing for honey, he soon discovered the bees he'd seen, could not have come from that tree, for when he pulled out his paw of honey it was covered with a swarm of bees.

Hughie dropped down from the tree running to get away as the angry bees chased him, but Bow stayed put until everyone was out of sight, then climbed the tree reaching in to get a big paw full of honey.

"I must not feel guilty!" she thought, "after all I did not even know them bees were in there," as she filled herself with honey, thanks to Hughie. By the time he got back she had honey smeared all over the front of her.

When Hughie came back, it was him following the bees instead of the other way around and they watched as they entered back into the hollow honey tree. Hughie had to be satisfied with what little honey he licked off Bow's face and chest, at least he'd get a little taste for his efforts, for he had no intention to make another try at the honey, telling Bow "you could have at least wiped more on yourself."

They were at mile forty on the Algoma Railroad and decided to cut across country to an old copper mine where Hughie went with his mother the year before. He knew of some swamps and old pine logs that had tasty frogs and carpenter ants.

Upon travelling down hills to the Achigan River on an old logging road, Hughie spotted a camping tent. He knew humans lived in these cloth tents and wondered where they were. Their car was there, but where were they? Were they fishermen or maybe prospectors?

If they were prospectors, they'd have food locked up in the car or have it tied in a tree somewhere, high enough so that bears wouldn't be able to reach it. Hughie and Bow looked all around and seen no bags tied in trees close by. Then they went to the car and nothing was locked inside. So they must be fishermen.

Bow said to Hughie, "let's go into their tent, if they are tourist fishermen, then they'll have sweets along hid in the tent somewhere. Let's go in and see what we can find before they get back Hughie."

The opening of the tent was zippered, so Bow then began to use her sharp claws, pulling down until she'd ripped a large hole in the material so they could walk in easily, these were inexperienced campers, they could tell because they'd left their food right out in the open instead of locking it up in their car.

The cardboard boxes were easily opened by tearing them apart, and the cookies were the first to be

Bow standing by Hughie, while Hughie has his head stuck inside of camper's tent.

Bow tosses a fish to Hughie on the river bank.

eaten, the strawberry jam was good, but the spice cake was the first Hughie ever had eaten and the sweet rolls were sticky, but good.

When they opened the little freezer, they were amazed at all the different kinds of meat it contained. Using their claws' they opened can after can of pop and beer, which squirted all over them and the tent, and they tasted them as they opened them, and some kinds tasted delicious!

The tent was in shambles when they were done with it, so great that an entire new camping outfit would have to be bought if they wanted to finish their vacation out doors. Hughie and Bow left through the same hole they'd made. As it turned out Bow spotted a pool of water under an old log bridge and they decided they'd freshen up a bit.

While they were in the pool the two fishermen came walking down the old logging road that led to the old copper mine, they had been up there fishing one of the lakes. The woman was the first to spot them in the pool of water.

She said to her husband, "Jim, look at the two bears, they are cute, aren't they? They seem to be having such fun and look at that one trying to catch a fish. Let me take time to take a picture of them. We may never be that close to two bears again. It'll be a nice picture to remember the trip by."

"That's a great idea," Jim said, "take several, they'll be nice to look back on." While they were snapping pictures, Hughie and Bow took off on the old logging road, to see what else they could find to do, after spotting the two taking pictures of them. They had no intentions of meeting the two of them or apologizing to them for the mess they had made to the tent.

Jim and his wife Ruth wandered over to their campsite, and when Ruth pulled down the zippered part, she let out one of the loudest screams that could stop a freight train. Jim came running for he didn't know what to think at the moment.

Once Jim was in the tent upon seeing the damage, he and Ruth clung to each other crying like little children. The two sweet bears were now called anything but sweet!

Both bears in a pool of water and the fishermen looking at them with admiration.

"If only that loaded camera would have been a loaded gun!" retorted Jim.

Ruth answered him in between sobs, "but we didn't know at the time they'd done all this damage, and we'd have killed two innocent bears. It just wouldn't have been right at the time."

"Well it's right now!" and they're long gone over the hill. Responded Jim, "besides I'd never catch them before dark. We'll just clean up this mess and sleep in the car tonight. Tomorrow we'll get a new camping outfit if I cannot get this tent repaired."

Better than that Ruth, let's just pack up and get a motel room in Sault Ste. Marie for tonight, that way we'll be right in town and can take our time shopping. Not only that I'll be able to take you out for a treat tonight, seeing you shot two bears with a camera. It's just a little humor, Ruth.

As for the two bears, they were long gone for places where they wouldn't be found. In that few minutes they were staring at Jim and Ruth they sensed that they'd done wrong, and took off for higher ridges.

Ruth and Jim took off for another area that was more populated, leaving the area to the rightful owners, the bears. As for Bow and Hughie they were far away from the trouble they had caused, however they stopped and decided to reminisce. It amazed them a little that with all the tasty food humans get to eat, why go out of their way to come up and eat what bears eat, like fish and wild fruit. They just couldn't understand.

Bow said, that jar of strawberry jam was so good, I just can't wait for another opportunity to get another jar

"Those jelly rolls were out of this world too!" remarked Hughie, 'but Bow, what about us? We wonder why the humans like our food, and listen to us brag about theirs, then they both burst out laughing.

Both of them travelled the bush for some weeks, Hughie met several other bears who tried to take his sweetheart away, but he held his ground in battle just like any human being would react, when someone tries to take their mate away. The only difference is, bears don't carry guns like some humans, which would be safer if they didn't.

Hughie finally found the time to tell Bow about his sister Honey being kidnapped and trapped by two men. To his surprise, she knew all about it, and she explained that his mother had told her mother one day at the Perry Creek.

Hughie was surprised as he didn't think they'd spent all that much time at the Perry Creek, then again maybe they had, after all, didn't Bow know everything, just like his mother!

One day while they were in the flatland where Honey had been kidnapped they came across a green pick up truck which he recognized as the same one used to take his beloved sister away. He knew the men were back to trap some unsuspecting bear, maybe even him. He told Bow not to stray too far away from him as he explained, and told her to stay close to him.

He could smell spoiled meat in the breeze, and by following the odor they came across the trap and the two men setting it. He told Bow if they were quiet they

Hughie recornizes truck in the flat lands where honey bear was kidnapped from.

could sneak up behind them and scare them away. At the moment the two were busy next to the beaver pond bent over, washing their hands and not paying a bit of attention to the backside of them.

Hughie whispered to Bow, "we'll walk very quietly toward them until we're about fifty feet away, then rush toward them growling, that ought to scare them well and they'll leave us be!"

Running and growling toward them, the two men were caught off guard, not even looking back, they jumped straight into the beaver pond landing in mud and water up to their necks.

It did Hughie good to see Honey's kidnappers struggling away in a bad situation themselves, made it difficult by their heavy shoes, and clothing.

While pushing their trap in place, they'd left their guns on the front seat of their truck. Hughie stood there on the bank of the pond intending to keep them in the water and mud just as long as he could, until he at least got even for his sister Honey bear, and what they did to her!

Hughie stood there with his teeth showing, growling deep from his throat. Bow was shocked with amazement as she saw him in action, and she now knew what a brave bear he was! She loved him all the more for wanting to protect his area and her, in what Hughie considered was GOD'S country.

Seeing the bears had made up their mind and were not going to give up so they could crawl up on the bank, they decided to try and make it to the other side of the pond. It was a hundred feet to the other side, and not an easy task dressed like they were. Hughie wasn't concerned with their problems, and so he held his ground.

Once the men reached the other side, they stood up on the other side shaking their fist and loudly yelling in a strange language the bears had never heard before. Hughie didn't seem to mind what language they spoke, at least they now knew just "who" was boss of the area! Hughie and Bow gave them a couple of last growls and took off for other things to do.

After all that excitement they found they were extra hungry and decided to go find some crawfish to eat. In the meanwhile the two men had decided to get across the beaver pond where they could get to their truck. They decided they would go a different way back, intending to dry out some.

They decided to walk to the beaver dam and cross over it, they found out it weren't easy to do for two reasons, especially if you were not sure a bear would step out of the bush, and try and cross on the same dam.

The limbs' beavers use for support to hold the dam together can get very slippery from age. Beavers use mostly poplar trees, chewing the bark off for food and using the tree for building the dam, so nothing goes to waste.

They were about halfway when one of the men lost his footing and over he went into the water, the other man was laughing up a storm when he too lost his footing! It just seemed there was no way they were going to dry out, regardless of which way they went. When this happened, they both burst into laughter, with tears running down their faces.

They both had to admit it as the best time they'd ever had in their field of their employment, trapping

Two Conservation Officers in the pond. Hughie and Bow standing on the pond's bank keeping the two men in the pond.

bears. Then they remembered that for a few minutes, the bears had them trapped, glad they didn't see us fall off the dam back into the pond or they'd have a good laugh over that.

As they pulled themselves out of the pond and slowly walked to where the bear trap was, they were both hoping there would be either bear in the trap, then again, what if both had been trapped? How would they ever manage to get them and the trap into the back of the truck, and would the hoist hold the weight of two bears?

Upon arriving at the trap their fears disappeared, there were not bears in the trap. What a relief it was to them being all wet and miserable and having no change of clothing with them, and from that day on they would be always carrying extra clothing along.

Talking as they walked one remarked, "I still say that the one bear is related to the one we had trapped in that prospector's cabin a few years ago, he is a mean one!"

"You don't suppose he is related to that she bear we got last fall, do you?" questioned the other trapper.

"I doubt it! If they came from the same litter, he'd have been travelling alone, I'm sure," said the other trapper.

"Well I won't argue with you, but I say you're wrong."

Finally the other said, "I think it's time to take the trap and find another area. I say this bear is too smart to come back. I know the smell of that meat drew them too quickly, or we wouldn't have been caught off guard like we were."

As they loaded and started to leave the area a skunk walked in front of the truck, crossing the road at a slow lazy pace, as he let up on the gas pedal, both men spoke at the same time. "Look even the other animals are rubbing it into us," and they both laughed as they then sped away.

"You know we have to make out our report, and one word gets around to the other men, we'll be the laughing stock of the crew."

"So what! Didn't we face the most clever two bears in the District of Algoma, and we should be honored to meet them that defend their territory? As far as I'm concerned, they won. Didn't they?" the one trapper stated.

"Oh you're right about that, but let's just keep it quiet as possible, okay?" he hated to think about the razzing they'd get.

* * *

CHAPTER 6

SHERIFF BEAR HUGHIE

Hughie and Bow were having the time of their lives catching frogs and crawfish as there was plenty wherever they'd go. Hughie was proud of himself, and when he was in a swamp everyone knew it for he'd stand on his hind legs as tall as he could send off a series of growls in all directions saying, "I always wanted to be a bear sheriff of Algoma, and I will put the run on all bad people who try to harm us and others!"

"You'll make a good sheriff Hughie," Bow replied, "but all humans aren't the same, look at the humans from the train who always throw goodies to us bears. If they knew we wanted to be mean, they wouldn't be so generous to us! You have to forgive to receive forgiveness Hughie."

"Just think Bow. I had those two guys right where I wanted them. Too bad I didn't ask them to throw us some speckle trout out of the pond before I let them go."

"I know Hughie, but you're not a bad bear like some are, you're my teddy bear."

"Will you quit saying that? I'm the sheriff of Algoma and not a teddy bear!"

"If you say so," remarked Bow, then she gave him a lick behind the ear.

"Hey, will you cut that out! That's no way to treat a bear sheriff when he's on duty."

Bow laughed to herself and said, "you're still my teddy bear, even if you made yourself the sheriff of Algoma."

A few days had passed when Hughie had another face off, only this time with one of his own kind. It seemed to him this other bear wanted Bow for "his" mate, and Hughie would have none of this nonsense. By chance they met on a beaver dam halfway and the battle began, they had a stand off for a couple of minutes, growling at each other. Then swiftly the attacks came with both bears standing up, toe to toe.

They grabbed each other like a couple of T. V. wrestlers do. They didn't have much room on that beaver dam and the wood was very slippery, all of a sudden they both fell into the cold pool of water and then each swam to the opposite side of the pond, and the fight was over.

Hughie swam to the shore where Bow was waiting and cheering him. She greeted him as the winner, and gave him a lick behind the ears as his reward.

Hughie did not reject her kisses this time for he had fought for her, and sort of felt he deserved this pleasure.

Hughie kept on avoiding the area where his sister had been kidnapped, because he had other things on his mind.

Hughie meets rival bear who wants to take Hughie's mate Bow away from him.

Soon the middle of Fall would be arriving, and he would help Bow find a good place to make a comfortable den, where they'd bed down for the Winter months. The color of fall also brought out a lot of tourists who would leave their food all over the place, wherever they had a picnic.

People love to see bears and to take pictures of them while at the same time thinking it was their duty to reward them with a handout, and so of course bears always expect a sweet tooth reward. One time a picnic was going on at the Whitman Dam and Hughie and Bow walked out of the bush as the breeze was blowing the aroma of barbecued chicken right to their noses. To them it meant dinner was ready to be served.

The couple having the picnic didn't invite nor expect any other company. Their van was parked near the barbeque pit and they were busy turning the chicken when the man looked up and saw two bears coming to dinner, uninvited, so telling his wife in a soft tone of voice, to go to the van and stay there, he then proceeded that way himself, and in his haste knocked over the grill and all the chicken went upon the ground.

He made it to the van all right, but wished he'd have grabbed some of the barbecued chicken that was done and his mouth watered as he watched Hughie and Bow enjoy not only the chicken, but other snacks they'd laid out.

Hughie and Bow watched them drive off down the road and wondered what their hurry was. Hughie and Bow had no idea that they were the ones who had scared the people off, they just thought it was because they already had their share of the chicken and was in a hurry to leave. A while later as the bears were leaving the camp spot, they saw the tourists return for their dining tools, and to put the fire out and they could smell the smoldering smoke as water was poured over it.

These are the good people who care, she reminded Hughie, because now there'll be no threat of a forest fire from their live coals they had left. Sure was nice of them to return and put them out.

Sheriff Hughie replied, "yes they are nice and were very thoughtful to leave us all that tasty chicken. Sure was good. I wish I had more, don't you Bow?"

Hughie and Bow drop in for lunch.

Although it was nearing hunting season the days were warm but the nights were cool, and it would be any day now that the deer hunters would arrive. He was afraid of American hunters most because they'd shoot a bear as well as a deer, Hughie didn't want Bow or him to end up as a trophy on someone's wall or as a bear rug on the floor.

The two bears found a good place for their den on the south side of a cliff, and out of the reach of any hunters. It was a perfect spot where they could see either way for long distances up and down the valley. As they were nearly finished collecting brush for the closure of the den, they spotted a group of hunters pulling in to set up their camp about a quarter of a mile away on the same side of the river where their den was to be. The bears could not only see them, they were so noisy they couldn't miss hearing them.

The following day they saw them crossing the river to look for deer run ways, and they left the camp unattended. Hughie watched them closely from the ridge on the cliff and saw them tie their boats to a tree, then climb up the bank with their guns in hand, and it wasn't even opening day yet. As they disappeared into the bush Hughie knew, they'd be gone all day.

Calling to Bow, "let's go out to dinner one last time before we close up the den for the winter, I believe I know a place where we can get a tasty meal down valley."

"What are we waiting for, let's go?" she cried out.

They walked into camp with no problem at all and crawled in under the tent. They soon found out that these were experienced hunters, there was nothing in the camp except for a few bags of cookies and potato chips, but these tasted all right. They then went outside and looked in the car through the window and seen boxes of can food, but no way to get into the cars. There was a U-haul trailer there, but this also was secured.

Hughie could smell meat somewhere. Looking up at a small maple tree he saw a bag tied to a limb. The tree was about three inches in diameter, and upon going closer the smell was stronger than ever. While the men had put polish sausage up there to thaw out for their supper that night after their scouting trip, Hughie wanted it now!

"I'll climb the tree Bow and when it bends close enough to the ground, grab it, then I'll jump down and help you."

Everything went along nicely, and they got the bag of frozen polish sausage and ran into the bush with it, after eating the sausage, they ran for the den and were now ready to close the entrance for their long winter sleep.

The hunters returned to camp and the first thing they discovered was their snacks were gone, they blamed it on another hunter passing through, since the tent wasn't damaged. After going to get the polish sausage down for their supper, they saw that the bag was gone and the bark on the maple was damaged with claw marks, they now knew a bear had taken the food from the tent also. Since there was no snow as yet they could not even track the bear who'd helped himself, and they blamed each other for not picking a bigger tree, not realizing that wouldn't have made any difference at all. Polish sausage to deer hunters is like porterhouse steak to a stockbroker, it's easier and more quickly prepared

Hughie climbs a small maple tree to lower the food sack to Bow's reach.

than porterhouse steak, and taste are delicious when you've been out in the fresh air all day. The deer hunters swore they were going to have bear steak before this hunting trip was over.

Hughie and Bow in their den were not quite that sleepy as they talked of their summer happenings, Hughie decided it was time to tell Bow the bear news he'd heard while he was at the dump one day. A mother bear told him her son had been captured, but had escaped from the zoo one day, he had seen Honey bear and spoken with her before escaping and she was doing just fine. She had her own mate there and two cubs. "Isn't that great, Bow? Wait until I someday see my mother and tell her she's a grandma bear now."

"Oh Hughie, I forgot to tell you, I saw your mother shopping at the dump one day and she already knows, I told her how happy we were too!"

"Hughie, what shall we do next summer? Are you still going to be the Algoma sheriff next year too? Do you think we'll have our own baby cubs like your sister Honey?"

"Hey slow down, you're just full of questions aren't you? Yes, I'm going to be the sheriff next summer, maybe always! It would be nice to have a couple of baby cubs, since I'm a sheriff I won't let any harm come to them and you can teach them how to take care of themselves, like my mother taught me. What would you like to do next summer, Bow?"

"You know Hughie, we've never even been near that place that's called, THE MOUNTAINS OF THE MIDWEST, at Searchmont. Can we go there? We can hide and watch the people who ski?"

Hughie laughed and said, "my crazy Bow, people don't ski in the summer time."

"Then, what do they do there?"

Hughie told her he'd heard from other bears that they do all kinds of things like, mountain biking, volleyball and even a circus, maybe Honey might even be there, but I have to tell you Bow, they don't have this until July, I was told. There will be more tourists who will be taking the train trip to Agawa Canyon, which means a lot of treats.

"I'm getting sleepy Hughie, so good night."

"I am too Bow, see you in the spring, my love."

THE END

BO-GIN ANIMAL NOVELS

The author, Boniface Idziak has written several manuscripts of the animal life he has encountered in the wilderness while on his prospecting ventures of the past 38 years.

His second novel of Hughie will be "Hughie and Bow," of their ventures as mates in the wilderness, concerning their heartaches and the taking up with their new friend Ruefus the bear, who Hughie had come into contact with before at the township dump, and had a standoff. A very humorous story and adventure into the lives of bears in the wilderness.

* * *